Monsieur GASSOON

A Novel by Marv Gold

Dedicated to Peter Ben Gold

ISBN 978-0-5781-5087-1

Copyright © Marv Gold, 2014

Published by Magi Books, 2015

WHAT PREVIEWERS ARE SAYING

"For aficionados of the art of the fart, Gold's novel never loses his sense of the gloriously absurd. Read this; contains no MSG or unnatural gas. For the literati he has perfected the Whoopie Cushion."

— *Raoul Metier, Artist*

"In this literary farce featuring the fart, Marv Gold's wacky words waft from page to page in a flurry of flatulent phrases. He takes the reader back in time to the Paris, France of the Fin de Siecle in an hilarious spoof that triggers chuckles, belly laughs and an occasional intestinal cramp from a suppressed flatus. His protagonist, Jean Vent-Jean, toots his derriere across the Belle-Epoque stage of the Moulin Rouge in the tradition of Le Pétomane. His musical farts are as odorless as they are tasteless. One would never guess that something so crass as rectal gas could inspire comedic prose. But Gold breaks with tradition as cleverly as Val-Jean breaks wind. *Monsieur Gassoon* is a must read for horn tooters everywhere."

— *Nino E. Green, Attorney*

"To know Gassoon is to applaud him, cheer him on to feats of greater fartissimo. And he does this by means of his one most versatile organ alone, his ass. In the novel *Monsieur Gassoon*, author Marv Gold examines the hypothesis that certain dietetic factors went into the alchemy that created his uproarious stomach. This comic novel examines the various causes of flatulence, and explodes a number of heinous myths."

— *Edna St. John, Realtor*

INTRODUCTION

Only the French would celebrate the end of a century as *le Fin de Siecle* . . . and at the same time the start of *la Belle Epoque*. Well, was it the end of loose, gay, wild merriment? Or a new era of loose, gay, wild merriment? Frankly, in 1900 it was both.

In that mixed up span came new Paris streets and sewers, the Eiffel Tower, new art and music, the Moulin Rouge—and a little comedian with one enormous talent, Jean Vent-Jean, and his musical bum. This is about a man who breezed his way to success.

The bony old donkey lunged, and hunching its shoulders, lurched up the rocky road step by step to the pass. Twenty steps away, fifteen more and he'd be there. Stretched out among the bales of hay in the back of the wagon, I couldn't help huffing with him. Perhaps another huff might help.

Did the donkey agree? Did he think about where it led? Tall, graceful sycamores, tinged with the scent of lavender and coastal breezes hinted at our nearing the sea. But why so many ruts and holes? How much farther? Ten more steps? Ah, and then it was clear sailing, down into the Provence valleys.

Yesterday I had hitched a ride aboard a passing hay rick, and by evening the sway-backed donkey had poked his way into the next valley. I have known many lovely summer mornings in many places. But never have I awakened to one so glorious as this.

By earliest dawn we had come past villages dotting the countryside, many quaint, charming, sleepy villages. Their names sounded alike; they stonily looked alike, possessing a church, city hall, produce market, a schoolhouse and stable, a pub and a dozen small shops.

In one such village on this summer's day the wagon clattered onto the cobble-stoned main street of Hyrer, and came to a halt in the village square. The old driver stood and called to me, nesting among the hay bales, "Up, up, *mon flaneur*! We are here!"

"All right!" I yelled back.

I sat up, shaded my eyes, and slammed a hat on my shapeless hair. "So we are, indeed. Bless you, my good man, for the ride."

"Then, off! Be off with you!" laughed the farmer, giving the reins a tug.

The donkey lurched forward, sliding me off the tailgate, practically tumbling me off.

I straightened my backpack, and plucking an orange from a fruit stand, I flipped a sou to the peddler, and shuffled on. Halfway down the narrow, stony street, I neared the village bakery and stopped to read the overhead sign. Boulangerie Piaget. The shop exuded pungent aromas of baguettes, rolls, tarts. But of course. Who else would be open so early?

I entered and flourished my hat a la a courtier.

"Bonjour, Papa!"

A cry went up from him, "Jesus, Mary and Joseph-— Jean! You are here!" He turned to his young sales clerks, "Girls! Your brother! Our prodigal is back! Coffee, please. For two!"

I bowed fancifully to my sisters, "Jean Vent-Jean, at your service."

Now commenced a cataloging of news. As the years unraveled, Papa listened to my travels—the boys' academy, the cadets, the Franco-Prussian trenches, the clochard years, and more recently, the theatrical years. It was colorful, an exciting mosaic of music hall life.

"And what is it you do on stage, Jean? You sing? You dance, tra-la?"

"Umnnno, Papa. Not exactly."

"Ah, of course. You play music— tootle the trombone, yes?"

I coughed, "You're close. But, um . . . not quite."

"Then I am puzzled. Are you a magician? A mime?"

"No, I am, uh . . . an entertainer. . .but . . ."

"But . . . what? What but?"

"That's right, Papa. I play. . . on my butt."

"Huh? You're serious? You make a living with your butt? How?"

"Well, . . ." I had to look around the shop.

Then I whispered, "I, umn . . . I fart."

Old Piaget slapped the zinc counter. "You fart? What is so thrilling about that? Everybody farts!"

"Yes, there are many amateurs, but only a true professional can fart the diatonic scale . . . "

I blew an octave of accurate notes,

"Do, re, mi, fa, sol, la, ti, do!"

Papa squirmed uneasily, *"Sacre bleu!"*

I volunteered to snap him out of it.

"Would you rather hear 'La Marseillaise'?"

Papa banged the counter, "Never! Not in my shop! You wouldn't dare fart the national anthem in my shop!

But I will tell *le monde*—You hear?

My son can fart songs! Operas! I've raised my son to be a musical fartiste!"

I sat through his sarcasm, eyes dimmed.

Papa was ranting, "Oh, is he different! You should pay to hear him! Even pay per smell!"

He was heaping it on. I put on my hat.

"Enough, Papa. Not funny. You make the *moquerie* of my career. I go!"

" Jean, Jean, wait! Yes, I poke fun. It is such an impudent crack-pot thing you do. Please. Maybe I do not understand today's entertainment."

I exhaled slowly.

"Let me explain," I began. "My work is comedy. It hinges on the embarrassment of farting. Most people are at a loss when they fart publicly. Do they apologize? Do they admit it? Never. Of course not. After all, a fart is a fleeting thing. A tickle of the bottom—then pouf! —a toot, a sniff, and gone. It comes, it goes, an apology would only call attention to it. Best to let it pass.

"After all, it stems from waste—a sodden, stinking, foul as shit, uncouth outrage. Oh, but what if the fart is noticed? Then the fun begins . . . in the ways we try to mask it — Some of us we blush, we sneeze and snuffle and stammer, some of us laugh or cough or blame it on others, and that part is funny! And when I do it on stage, it's a riot. Everyone considers it somebody else's *faux pas*, and they scream, they roar. And so, what I do . . . becomes funny! Get it, Pop? It's entertaining!"

"What? The audience never gets upset? By the smell? They never want to tar and feather you?"

"Oh, I've flopped once or twice. But there is no smell because there is no gas. Only air . . . and their imaginations. More often they demand encores—they want to see the tenor, a soprano, a tuba player, especially a ballerina rip one off. Oh my lord, how they roar! They laugh, they cry in the aisles! Laughter to the rafters! And why? Because their wish has come true! And for this, they are willing to pay through the nose! Now do you get it?"

Papa pondered, then slowly nodded.

He whispered, "Magic, pure magic. You've got a goldmine in your ass—if— if you can keep it up! For an audience, for who knows, a career!"

"Ah, then you do understand," I said, patting his hand. "Because I have kept it up for six years. And God willing, I shall continue. Which is exactly why I came to you today."

"Ahaaa . . . Yes, Jean. I've been wondering."

Piaget scraped the crumbs from the table. "Why did you come?"

"You know, Papa, I travel a good deal around France. And my life is not always a bed of roses. Little expenses here, expenses there, it adds up. Frankly, Papa, I can use a helping hand."

"Yes, I can imagine. I noticed the hay wagon passing by, the straw on your coat. Well, I'd help if I had two centimes to clink together. But my shop I fear is a lost cause. The ladies here, bless them, they bake their own bread. They grind their own flour. They have their own recipes. That leaves me betwixt and between.

"Betwixt? . . . between what?"

"Just an expression. Better if you could look behind the eight ball and the bank, and you would see me . . . way behind both!"

I bit my lip. Damn, I'd done it again. Come to the wrong man at the wrong time and place. That left me and my ass out in the cold, unless . . .I could try one last roll of the dice.

"I understand, Papa, You are indeed a modest man. But such a baker as Provence has never known. A born baker. A king among bakers."

"I thank you, my son. Of course. I do bake the best croissants, the best cakes most certainly. But remember, in my youth I was a musician. I played all the strings—from the lute to the harp, piano, zither. Do you remember my lute?"

Reaching under the counter, Piaget tenderly showed a small mandolin-like instrument. He slapped and strummed it, "You see? As good as ever."

I was stunned. Papa had just hooked himself. An egotist forever. What a wonderful accomplice the ego is. "Yes, I remember. And that is why I am so sure we can be a success."

"We— a success? *Piaget et Fils?* It would be a great bakery! Of course, you will have to learn to bake—"

"Ta ta, wait, Papa. I'm talking about you joining my business. This can be a splendid partnership."

"Doing what? The two of us singing and farting on stage? Not me, my son. Forget it."

"Nossir, the entertaining is what I do. You'll be the manager, the agent, the publicist and the treasurer. Mr. Executive, the front man of our company. And I'll perform for our company. Together we mesh, left hand and right. We can't miss, *mon pere*."

"Jean, I love you, you talk the good game. But this is a gamble with huge risk. I stand to lose everything. My business, my investments, home, my wife and family, my good name among neighbors and customers. I could be ruined."

"And I too. Whatever we do, whichever way we go will always have risk. But as two good entrepreneurs, we share the goldmine as you called it, and we can make a fortune. So how about it, Papa? Do we go under? Or shall we shake and make a go of it?"

"I say, . . yes, my son! We make a go of it. For one month, while I see how it works. How I can contribute. How much we earn. Then we'll sign the papers and make it official. A name. What shall we call the business?"

Papa had no idea, "But not Piaget et Piaget, no real names. How about a name for our attraction? "The *Fartzer*!" (I frowned.) "No? Then the *EnFarceur*?" (I frowned again.) "Maybe *The Farceur*?" This also drew a *moue*'.

Alors I quietly said, "Ahem, there is a name. A name that says it all, a name I can work with as a polished performer. It is (pause) . . . "Monsieur Gassoon."

The old man sat back, reflecting. He sucked his pipe, trying out the name. Then he smiled. "Why not? Yes, Jean, it is a good name. But I still ask, can it be done? How can we be sure?"

"We will become sure as we go. As we make an effort and count our francs. It will be easy as pie. Watch my eyes, and visualize the Franco-Prussian War."

I hitched up my pants, and bent forward.

"Try to remember that war. It started with rifles (BLOWS WEAK POPGUNS). Pretty soon we needed cannons on wheels. We needed tanks! Charge! (HE BLASTS CANNONFIRE). And how about a giant of a cannon on a railroad train, Hefty Hilda! With a trajectory of two miles. Ready, aim, fire! (BLOWS A MASSIVE EXPLOSION!) So Papa, will we get this done?"

The old man was overwhelmed. He raised his cup. "I say, onward Christian soldiers! Farting as to war!"

In the back room, he gathered a few belongings on a bindle stick. He gave Margot his key ring and said, "For one month, *mon cherie*. For one month, you are in charge. I am off to see Paris! With my son! Toodley–oo."

The Open Road

Hiking down the narrow valley road, I sketched out the next few weeks. "Our plan is fourfold: The product, the market, the tools, the income. The product you know. The tools are our props—certain instruments, tubing, you'll see. Our surprise is the low comedy of *Le Fart*. The first major market is Marseille.

Route 57 to Marseille is a short way, about 40 kilometers. A busy road dotted with small towns. Our act will have to move like a domino through pubs in Toulon, Tamaris, Pepiole, La Seyne, Beaucaire, and so on."

"Initially, our market will be men, working class men. They flock the pubs after hours. They have the free time, they like earthy humor, and they have the loose change to contribute."

"In each town we search out the busiest pubs. At each pub I will perform the act, welcome donations, and we move on. Two shows per night could net us a hundred francs daily."

Papa agreed: "Why, in two weeks we could clear as much as twelve hundred francs. And besides, we would approach Paris with a polished act."

"Correction, Papa. A dozen appearances in Lyon can put us on our way. Then we can splurge a bit for new outfits, travel by train, enjoy better meals and lodging, and find ideal venues, those doing a lot of publicity. How much can our expenses be? A few taxis, room and board. Not very much."

And so, on our first night on the road, we wandered through the heavy trucking districts looking for suitably crowded taverns. Hoisting his small lute over one shoulder, Papa would humbly enter a pub, and order a short beer. The patrons would scrutinize him, and after awhile, he'd start up some conversation.

"*Bonsoir*, my compliments on your weather."

"*Bonsoir* and beware. You are a musician? Toulon does not take too kindly to strangers." A barrage of questions followed from the crowd around the bar. "Do you fish? You have a boat? Who do you know here?"

He said he was here to meet Monsieur Gassoon, a friend from Marseilles. "Garcon? A boy? Who's that? What's his line of work?"

"Gassoon, my good man. And I believe he does imitations. Ah, here he is."

I entered the pub, wearing my black slouch hat and cape. Papa said. "*Bonsoir*, Jean. Gentlemen, meet Monsieur Gassoon." The usual congenialities were exchanged, and questions asked.

"From Marseille, eh? We hear you do imitations, Garzoon." Some were curious, some eager to witness my act. I was, of course, most obliging.

"Have a cognac on us."

I slipped off my cape, looking well groomed, a clean shirt, shined shoes. With a pleasant nod I introduced myself to the men at the bar.

"*Bonsoir, mes amis*. Yes, I am Monsieur Gassoon. Perhaps you have heard of me, perhaps not.

No matter, *Salud*! You certainly know how to welcome a wayfarer . . ."

They joined Papa in an agreeable mood. "Thank you. You will see no tricks, for I am not a magician. I make sounds on the lowliest of wind instruments, but one that I have mastered. And I trust you will have a jolly good time. *N'est-ce pas?*"

Without further ado, I proceeded into my act "First, gentlemen, let me ask. Are you aware of women's voices?" Immediately they hooted, "Are we?

Ho, ho!' . . . "Are you kidding?". . ."All depends, which woman?" ... "How much wine she's had!"

"Then listen up, gentlemen. And you will hear women as you've never heard them. First listen to a pert young girl on her first date." I showed them my tiny harmonica. I bent forward, inserting it into my rectum, I showed my empty hand, strained a moment, and smiled, (MAKING A GIDDY, BUBBLING SOUND).

The men froze. "Who farted?. . . Did you?. . .What the Hell?"

"Yes," I said, "It was me. And now imagine she's at the altar being wed, expressing her true devotion." (CLASPS HANDS IN PRAYER, MAKES SOLEMN SOUNDS). Most of them laughed. But others pointed at my rump. I smiled, validating their accuracy.

"At last it is the honeymoon night." (COOING, SEXUAL SOUNDS). This time the crowd fully understood—and the wolf calls began, the whistles and laughter.

"But soon the honeymoon is over and the marriage gets down to business. (A LOW, GROWLING SOUND)." Their laughter went out of control. The men guffawed, stomped, barked.

"Years pass and Mama becomes a mother-in-law: "(FEROCIOUS LION SOUNDS).

At this the crowd exploded into peals of laughter and growls, and I thanked them, "Yes, gentlemen, these are but farts in the night. But to the discerning, one good fart deserves another. Thank you for your attention. And if you care to contribute a few francs to our sustenance, it will be most appreciated."

On that note, we extended our caps in the classic bow, and that did it, cracked up the group.

"Haw! Some sustenance, fellas! He means beans!" The laughter subsided for a few more comic vignettes, and after awhile Papa and I were ready to call it a night, our success borne out by well-filled caps.

The tour was gratifying. Papa was elated. I had put on a good act, and the first few towns had paid us adequately, especially for the follow-up encores. This new venture had some possibilities. But how would it fare in Lyon and among the Paris sophisticates?

At the next town, our introductions went smoothly, and I thought I'd practice some variations.

"For instance," I said, "We are all fond of dogs, are we not?"

"Consider the Pekingese. He may be small, but he can make quite a noise." I then shifted into my bent forward stance, and emitted a squealing (PEEP, PEEP, PEEP SOUND). As before, the first reaction was bewilderment, "What the hell? A dog fart?"

"Next we have the ever-frisky terrier," (SOUND OF LIVELY YAPPING). This time the men chuckled.. Some called out, "Hey, that's no terrier. It's his *derrière!*"

"But do some of us prefer a larger companion? Then we own a German Shepherd," (LOUDER BARKING OF A WATCHDOG). One wise-guy screamed, "Watch out! His butt may attack us!" This time the crowd went wild.

"Yes, in my kennel, I do have an enormously brave dog, that wonderful Swiss rescuer, the St. Bernard." (LOW GUTTURAL COW-LIKE WOOFING). The reaction was electric. Dozens of grown men were baying, barking at each other. They settled down for a few more vignettes, and after awhile Papa and I were ready to call it a night, our success sustained by well-filled caps.

We waved good night, thanking them for their encouragement and their kind contributions.

Apparently, word of mouth carries among small towns. Some word of our act had preceded us into Marseille, so I didn't have to explain my unique talent or our mission. We found we could play directly into their interests. "As a veteran, let me review our war with the Prussians. As you remember, we were sent to the front lines with what? Pistols? (PING PING SOUNDS.)

Here audiences laughed, and I added, "We needed rifles. And what did we get?"

"Peashooters! (LOUDER FIRING, RICOCHETS.) Slingshots are better!

"Our generals realized we needed cannons. Ready! Aim! But did we ever fire?" (HOWITZER-LIKE CANNONFIRE, FIZZLING EFFECT).

Ah, but finally came air power! We armed our barrage balloons with bombs: (SLIDEWHISTLE DESCENDS, EXPLOSIONS).

Until at last by 1871, we realized that our aerial warfare was a dud. It didn't cut the mustard. (A DWINDLING SPIRAL AND A THUD).

The laughter among the veterans was wild, riotous and rampant. This brought a few raucous raspberries from the crowd for which I saluted them.

Now it was time to wrap up. "Some of you may wonder how I achieve this fantastic fartistry. Please notice that at no time do I use a wind machine, or any tricks, or do my hands touch my pants."

" I eat no special foods, no beans, cabbage, or radishes. And these are not fake noises. They actually do come from my *heinie*. All are real farts you can do as I do, with no odors, in any loudness. And if you wish, you may now contribute to our training and travels as we pass the hat. I thank you, *bonsoir*."

Then for encores, I played real tunes on several instruments. A harmonica, a kazoo, an ocarina, a flute. And a bagpipe with no knee or elbow action. "These," I said, "are not toys, and not to be taken lightly; they are genuine musical instruments. And while I did not know a note of music, nonetheless I can play them by rear."

That night, after all the applause, and after two shows my cap was full of much more than 400 francs. Papa and I knew we had quite a good start.

I sat down with a pencil and paper, and wrote out my lines, listing the continuity of my presentations and the content. Above all, the tone must always be upscale, courteous, and in good taste. This manifesto became our style sheet, and part of our working contract.

Within nine days we were in Marseille. One night I did "The Lark," a well known lullaby:

Alouette, gentille alouette,

Je te plumerai la tête.

Et la tête! Et la tête!

Alouette! Alouette!

A-a-a-alouette

There were eight verses in all, and I played them with my complete collection of anal instruments.

At Lyon

Three more towns and some pronounced frugality put us 1200 francs ahead. Moving into Lyon, we heard a ruckus from one pub, The Green Pomegranate. It would be our target, while lining up one more for the late show. Papa sauntered in, and up to the bar. He showed two fingers to the innkeeper, "A small *Courvoisier*, please," As he had another, a few men greeted him.

"And what brings you to Lyon?"

"Ah, probably sentiment, an old flame. I'm thinking of settling down."

At that moment the door pushed open and I came in. I introduced myself, gave my rehearsal story and we did our usual early show. Casually thanking the customers, Papa passed the hat, and collected many francs. Then we took a recess, "We'll be back."

Between shows we had dinner at a nearby small bistro.

We sat at a corner table, and sipped rich dark coffee with liqueur, reviewing our first day in Lyon. Our easy, relaxed mood, and smiles said it all; we had made good progress.

"And if we continue our plan, without too many hitches, like a mistral, or getting sick or a riot or flood—why, we should go on amassing more francs."

"Yes, Jean, I'm beginning to see daylight as we go. As often as I've seen your act, I'm still astonished."

"All I can say is, it's a gift. A personal gift, which I accept without question or quibble."

"But from whom? A teacher? A classmate?"

"Some things we are not meant to know; they simply happen. After all, who created Lourdes? Stonehenge? We really don't know. I am simply thankful this happened to me."

"But how does it work?"

"All I can really know is my process. As you've seen, I do it in steps—

Step ONE: I exhaust all air from my lungs, and block any further inhaling.

Step TWO: I consume big gulps of air, four gulps. These I only draw in through my arse.

Step THREE: I store them in my large intestine in layers, four separate layers.

Step FOUR: I call up each layer as needed. How? Well, like regurgitating. Urp-urp-urp.

Only my anus muscles are able to urge each layer to surface.

Step FIVE, ejection: You've seen me bend forward. My sternum is pressing my intestines, firing out of my anus one layer at a time. And I can limit it, I can vary it. For a high note I tighten my butt. For a low note I loosen the butt muscles. And it has no odor at all. It's air... pure air."

Papa was still mystified. "B, but . . . where did you learn this?"

"I don't know, I stumbled onto it. Or I should say it found me— one summer years ago at school."

It was growing late, and we were both very tired, so the idea of sleep had become appealing. As I blanked out, a recurring dream took over.

I was about twelve and I was back at the academy, sailing a little boat, a skiff out of the harbor when I saw storm clouds. A big one was on the way.

A hurricane? A mistral? The wind was rising sharply, a cold piercing wind, flapping and billowing the sail.

Well, as an able-bodied seaman I had sailed into winds before. But never into rain and a rising squall like this! When the skiff started creaking and groaning, that's all—

I was sure the skiff would be swamped. I wound down the main sail. I searched a locker for oars, floats, a flare; but the cupboard was bare. I had no time to waste. With a curse, I bailed out, swimming for shore.

Fighting a rip current, my limbs felt leaden. If I could roll over on my back; I might be able to rest on the salt water. Floating calmed me and I inhaled, spitting out mouthfuls of sea water. It was hopeless. I was making no headway, I looked out toward the crashing thunderheads, the distant pier. I ground my teeth.

Damn! Now of all things, it started to pour!

I waved and called to the boys on the beach. They were running for shelter, their voices whooping, their laughter cresting above the waves. Would they look for me? How? They couldn't even hear me.

The wind turned cold, it raked across my wet body. I was trembling. Why had I chosen so stupid a course? Had I been daydreaming? Was I mistaken? What if I was swept out to sea by the current? I shuddered. I could drown out here and nobody would know.

Would they remember me, look for me? Find me? Would my trunks still be on? Would I look pruny blue? What'll my parents, my family say? Would my casket be open? Would I get a churchyard burial? What could my headstone possibly say?

That I was twelve, more or less? That I was a student? No trade, no profession. Would it say I was a nobody? That this time I had gone out too far? I looked around. I would never make it back.

The buoys were clanking goodbye, goodbye. Salt water was clutching at my throat, leaking into my lungs.

I couldn't help it; I wept, the drowning had begun.

I shivered. No! Wait, not yet. Not me, the best swimmer in my dorm. Wait! I inhaled a large swallow of air, with some seawater. If only I could gather up, rally one hoarse cry. If only one boy heard me.

Then they'd come. They'd rush in to save me. Yes, if they heard me! But the waves, the wind and rain. The boys howling and hooting. I'd never be heard.

My only hope came down to me, my will and stamina, my faith in my strength, my prayers, *"Mon Dieu*, help me! Help me kick and stroke. *I want to live!"*

And so, gritting my teeth, my body shivering with every stroke, I gave it my all. Grunting aloud. Pressing on with my whole body. Slogging my way toward shore. Inhaling bigger volumes of air, gagging on the icy gulps stabbing my chest.

Suddenly, from nowhere, out of the blue— came a burst of energy! It startled me, it seemed to gather and roll in my stomach. What the hell? Was it a wave, some invisible force? Prodding me toward a beach dotted with blankets, open umbrellas, tents, beach huts.

Then came a full surge. A long drawn out rumble seized me, and was hurling me toward land! "What is it, the Devil's breath?" I wondered. "My gut!" I howled. My butt was discharging! If so, then two can play!

I'd roll with it. Time myself, wait for a second wind. Then propel myself, stumble forward. Make my feet go churning, racing toward shore.

Ah, I could feel it in my toes. Scraping gritty muddy sand, sloshing through layers of kelp, algae, touching wet terra firma. An ominous growl retched at my innards. Nausea? Gas? A belch? It swelled and expanded in my stomach, Then my bladder—was this saltwater? I was only thirty feet from shore, within reach, within grasp, when it hit me—

A sudden, powerful burst blasted my bum, uplifting me ashore, jetting me over sand banks and onto a grassy rise. I lay there curled up, sobbing, trembling, breathing heavily, trying to catch my breath. Friends and classmates dashed over.

"Jean!"..."Are you all right?"..."*Mon Dieu*, what happened?"

"How'd you ever get ashore?"

I sat up and showed my feet littered with seaweed, roots, stems.

"Jean! You are a walking toilette!"

I could not stifle it any longer.

Suddenly the internal mass combusted, "Baarrrɔooom!"

A blast of gas followed by a jet stream of water

"Look at the seaweed he farted!"

"What the hell was that, Jean?"

"I don't know! . . . But it got me here."

"A fart?. . . saved your ass?"

Was it all sixteen years ago? 1 remember it indelibly. In the war I'd had several close calls, but this scare plays over and over. It has formed my character, given me persistence.

The next weeks were even more exciting. We did more shows, adding a few extra twists like mind-reading, magic. Late one night Papa and I had a nightcap or two, and put on a grand show. We had accomplished phase one—starting from scratch we had amassed six thousand francs. Enough to leapfrog to Paris.

C'est ca Paris

Any first morning in Paris is unbelievable. To newcomers it can be likened to uncorking a new wine. The fragrance enchants, the bouquet drifts.

It hovers over a solitary browser walking the Quay de Montebello to a lonesome blues beat. It has much the mood following an all-night party. Drained, wiped out, light headed.

Soft blue dawn creeps up hillsides, casting long shadows on garden walls, glimmering across wet cobble-stones and steps, dew glistening on linden trees, maybe a vendor or two starting the day. This day in 1898 appeared softly sumptuous.

What I remember most about Paris on this first day was an amazing morning feeling. The promise of wide-open possibilities. It might have been something in the air, the way it gently blew, even the way it tasted, crisp and minty. There was a golden gloss to the light, and a Sunday morning peace to the city.

Was this all my imagination? Not quite, for Paris was undergoing *le Fin de Siecle.*

The end of a gilded century, and mounting a replacement era, *La Belle-Epoque* with new housing and architecture, a world's fair and industrial exposition, new schools of music and art.

We could feel it as we set out from the Arch de Triomphe to the star streets, exploring the grand boulevards. Puncturing the horizon, a skeletal framework was rising, an iron tower designed by a French bridge-builder. Nearby along the Seine was another new structure, the Musee d'Orsay. For many years it had been the Paris terminal for the busy Orleans railway line. By 1900 it was to be razed. But French frugality begat ingenuity and saved it, transforming it into a brilliant art museum.

We toured the Place des Vosges, the Louvre, and the Luxembourg Gardens, getting the lay of the land. Jauntily strolling down the Champs Elysees we headed toward the Jardin des Tuileries, turning north onto the Place de la Concorde to angle toward the Opera Guarnier, discussing our plans as we walked.

Almost magnetically we came to the Place Pigalle at the foothills of Montmartre, and looked over the many bars, cabarets, and pubs celebrating the turn of the century.

Here in one plaza were the Folies Bergere, Cyrano's, La Chat Noir, Le Cave, many nightclubs. And one overpowering structure. Where the Boulevard de Clichy intersected Place Blanche, rue Fontaine, and rue Bruxelles, looming six stories high stood a soaring replica of a giant red grain mill. One look at its slowly turning sails and Papa was in awe.

"I think . . . I think we are at the Moulin Rouge."

I laughed, "It's turning in the wind . . . greeting us."

A little look-see seemed in order, so we bought tickets for the day's matinée.

The lobbies well befitted an opera house. They were grandiose, furnished with marble staircases, thick carpeting, rococo balustrades, columns, sculptures, fresco ceilings.

Entering the main room we saw hundreds of beautifully dressed dinner tables and a dazzling horseshoe of private dinner booths. Shown to our table, we noted the excellent sightline to the stage and the red velvet seating. The stage is a vast wall-to-wall dance floor, gleamingly waxed, and colorfully lit by roving spotlights, It was surrounded by galleries of mirrors, perhaps not as many as at Versailles, but very resplendent.

Casually the main show room was filling with patrons.

Ordering the 189 *franc prix fixe* three-course dinner, we were pleased that it included a bottle of premium champagne. As we admired the wonder of the setting, the orchestra finished tuning up, and settled back, awaiting a cue. The baton tapped twice, and with a cymbal crash, the orchestra swung into a blazing Offenbach fanfare. Out stepped Monsieur Oller, the master of ceremonies, and in flawless French and English greeted the audience.

"*Bienvenu*! Welcome! Honored guests, men and women! Le Moulin Rouge, the world-famous dinner nightclub is pleased to present our show of shows, the best entertainment that Paris has to offer.

"Today, you will be entertained by the ever-appealing Maurice Chevalier, the romantic Sara Bernhardt, our inimitable little sparrow, Edith Piaf and yes, our playful Mistinguette. You will hear the latest sophisticated show tunes as played by Jules Duvivier's Moulin Rouge orchestra, and you will see, wonder of wonders, the Doriss girls! Sixty of the world's most exciting can-can dancers—and now, get ready to be amazed! For Here They Are!"

The orchestra broke into a brassy song, the backdrop quickly spun open to an ornate, lavish extravaganza setting—

Suddenly they appeared! Thirty gorgeous girls were throwing themselves at us in a high-kicking, skirt-flourishing can-can! Their fast, wild entrance was exhilarating!

They circled the floor, spinning their skirts, nodding and flashing smiles at each patron, forming an aisle for their leader's grand entrance. The backdrop flashed open again, revealing a crystal stairway as La Goulue came skipping down in highly revealing, skimpy lingerie, followed by another thirty dancers. They whipped through several can-can sets and danced off to cheers . . . as the M.C. stepped out to introduce the biggest singing star in Paris.

To a tympani drum roll . . . Chevalier himself came forward!

He waved and bowed, he greeted friends and dignitaries by tipping his signature straw hat. This he happily spun out to the crowd as he launched into his popular song "Louise!" The audience cheered wildly as his straw hat came sailing back. In thanks he pouted his well known smile, and then ramped into "Mimi," "Valentina," and "Prosper." Each song bringing him into an embrace and two-step with another Doriss Girl.

And so it went, singer after singer, after jugglers, acrobats, aerialists, mimes, horses and magicians, until they reached the peak of the show. (Or dare I call it a circus?) And then it again became a whirling devil-may-care can-can. Only perhaps a bit more devilish, in that the girls did some stripping. They kicked off their lingerie to the oglers, and the first kick of their nude limbs brought the house down. It was pure mayhem with elderly gents tossing their top hats to the dancers, and squealing ladies touring the tables kissing their bald pates.

Of course, it remained for La Goulue to restore order. With her entire chorus line of sixty Doriss can-can girls, she sang a warm closing song. "Good night, and *á bientôt* ..."

Afterwards, Papa and I, both overcome and drained, staggered outside.

Completely exhausted, we sought a bracer at a Pigalle brasserie, and rested up with two wonderful liqueurs. Having come this far, we were more eager than ever to crash the Moulin Rouge and set Paris on its rump. "Was this still our plan?"

"Yes," I said, "and for the Rouge, we'll need terrific clothes, both costumes and everyday." We found a tailor shop on Avenue Emile Zola that specialized in theatrical wear.

I wanted some highly stylized evening wear—a long black satin tuxedo jacket with tails, some knee-length red satin breeches (specially rear-tailored). A gold brocade vest. A white bloused poet's shirt. A loose black cravat. Long ribbed white stockings, white gloves, a gold watch fob, and elegant high gloss Richelieu gold color buckled black patent leather pumps topped by ivory spats. In one little shop and one visit we found it all, and had gone beyond the reaches of theatrical fashion. To a touch of class, dignity.

"Later, we'll need pseudo nurses, perhaps four of them armed with ammonia inhalers, ice packs and stretchers. Nearby on Boulevard Clichy we may find a casting agency that provides temp help to theatres: young ladies not necessarily nurses, but able to perk up patrons who become over wrought. And for mood music, introductions, fast rhythms and accents, we'll need a few musicians to play piano, drums, guitar, and bass. And these too can be hired as we go."

"Of course, we'll need private rehearsal rooms and the Bateau-Lavoir near the rue Abesseses in Montmartre seemed to fill the bill properly. Here we can mix with Braque, Toulouse-Lautrec, Modigliani and Utrillo for publicity and hand-out souvenirs.

"The main question is how to publicize so vulgar an act? How to upgrade it? And how to convey that this act is unbelievably funny, in good taste and worth the expense.

"Clearly we will need something more—the excited curiosity of the public, a spread of newspaper stories and much word-of-mouth, perhaps radio interviews without giving away the gist of our act. Let them guess at our content for awhile. In time, of course, with growing attendance our secret will become known.

"So radio and word of mouth, the popular grapevine become important. These we must begin immediately, and run heavily for one week. At which point we will converge upon the Moulin Rouge and score play dates.

"Let's get started with public media. I'll see about interviews. Papa, you'll contact all print media—newspapers, gazettes, reviews, such as, *France Soir, Le Monde, Diapason, Art Presse, Beaux Artes, Pariscope, Le Figaro, Boulevard*, and *L'Officiel des Spectacles*."

Meanwhile I began rehearsing for my interview with Monsieur Oller, founder of the Moulin Rouge.

As I saw it, whether he's a tough old buzzard or a teddy bear, I will have to present something that will instantly capture his attention. A stunt? A personality? A demonstration? A deal? Perhaps an eye patch?

I must be brimming with confidence.

Accordingly, the next morning wearing my cape over my full stage outfit I entered the outer office of the Moulin Rouge director. Without pause I simply sauntered through the entry gate and past the gate-keepers.

I am here, I declared, for my appointment with Monsieur Oller, and he insists I be on time.

(Not a bad line, though completely bogus.)

With that I kept moving and entered Oller's office. He looked up from his desk. Taken aback by my intrusion (and cape and manner), Oller licked his dry, cracked lips and reached for his monocle. Drawing a bead on me, he drummed his pencil. I whipped off my cape with a full display of my costume.

I stood at attention and announced, "*Bonjour*, Monsieur Oller. I am here at last—Monsieur Gassoon, a headline act from Lyon. And I am ready for an audition towards an engagement at your Moulin Rouge."

Oller managed to gasp, "Oh? And who sent you here?"

"Everyone who has seen me. They all say I belong here."

"Oh? I see . . . They want you here? But not there?"

(Oops, no comeback for that. Best to just shut up.)

Oller licked his dry, flecked lips. His sarcasm dripped.

"How kind of them. How profoundly kind. And they told you to . . . intrude on me?"

"No sir, and I do apologize."

"Then let me tell you, Monsieur Garcon . . . The Moulin Rouge auditions no one— we don't have to. If you're a star, we contact you!"

"Good. Then I am ready for contact. I can perform right here, if you like."

(Careful. His temper was brewing. Also my gas was brewing.)

Oller stood up dramatically at his desk, "Before you do that, sir, please to get your ass out of here. I said no auditions."

(A buzzard? A teddy bear? He's more like a grizzly.)

"Yes, I heard. You hire stars, *et la*! Today, here I am!"

Oller snorted a laugh, "Damn, you are dogged. But. . . perhaps there is a way.

Tomorrow night. Play our outdoor pavilion, the Elephant Garden. Without pay, of course, until we have a contract."

"Of course. This Elephant show will be better than an audition."

"Oh? How so?"

"It is my debut."

Oller laughed. "Or a shitflop. Either the Elephant's trunk goes up and he follows you. Or his tail goes up and you follow him, with the shovel."

"Ugh, I'll watch my step," I said, getting a chuckle from M. Oller.

"When shall I show up?"

"For rehearsing or special music, be here at six tomorrow. Otherwise be here at 7:30.

The Elephant starts at 8 o'clock!"

Oller sank back into his leather chair and pointed to the door.

"Now, *monsieur, bonjour*! Please to barge out!"

And that was it. Not exactly magic, but not bad. Monsieur Oller seemed cautious. But did he ask about the nature of my act or my gaudy costume? No. He really was testing my mettle, trying me out, completely in the dark. Very unusual.

L'Isle de St. Louis

Papa looked down at the Seine, resting his chin on the railing of a cast iron bridge. It was the Pont de l'Archeveche, the pedestrian bridge for lovers.

Lord, he needed a good night's sleep. He was exhausted. Having made the rounds of Paris gazettes and journals, and introducing Monsieur Gassoon as a comic novelty act, his news received yawns and snorts.

So he invited the editors to the Elephant Garden tonight.

Looking to far horizons, he wondered. How did God do it? Create this island called Paris? This L'Isle de France in the rush of the Seine? And in its wake a thin islet, L'Isle d'St. Louis. Colonies in a file, conjoined in a single stream.

The old man gazed at the row of lovers' padlocks hooked to the bridge. He gently hung his cane in one of the railing curlicues. A launch passed below, a flat bottom bateux-mouche barge on the rushing waters, its lights flooding ghostly riverside buildings. Furtively the old man unbuttoned his coat. Gaiety, songs, party laughter arose from below. Some couples waved "thumbs up" to the old man.

He grabbed his crotch, "*Bonjour* yourselves! Look closely, and you will behold the remnants of the grand *Fin de Siecle. Bas a'ici!*"

Suddenly he was clutched at the elbow—

"Wait, sir! *Arretez*! Don't do it!"

"What it?" he grumbled. "What is it I shouldn't do?"

Holding his sleeve was a young woman. Tearfully, she clung to him.

"You mustn't jump! Please, sir! *Arretez!*"

The old man pulled away, "Jump? I'm lucky to be walking. But jump in the Seine?

Ha! You must be joking."

He muttered, straightening his coat. "The nerve! *Une fois* a gentleman could pee where he chose, in the street, the river. Who cared? Nobody was upset!"

"Oh, I am sorry—" she said. "You scared me."

The old man nodded politely.

"*Noblesse oblige,* my dear. Let us *oublier* about jumping. Instead, may I invite you to join me in some hot *chocolat?*"

She hesitated a moment, then re-sensing it, smiled.

"Well, maybe. Until my Gerard shows up,"

She smiled and slung her book bag over her shoulder. Behind Notre Dame's buttresses they found a grassy square and a vacant bench. Here a vendor poured them steaming drinks.

"My name is Leona. But please, I prefer Lee."

"And everyone calls me 'Papa'. . . though I much prefer Henri. Then you are *Americain?*"

"Yes, studying at L'Ecole des Beaux Artes."

"Ahh, an *artiste.*"

"Some day, I hope. You can tell?"

"Your fingers tell me—a dab of cobalt blue, cad red. A second year student, yes?"

"Yes, and you? You are an *artiste?*"

"I dabble after a fashion. I, um. . . dabble in the performing arts."

"Really? Might I see your work?"

The old man laughed, "I doubt it. It is as fragile as . . . the wind."

"Then what arts do you perform?"

"You'll never guess."

"I'd say . . . juggling?"

Henri smiled, "Flattering, but no."

"A magician? A mime?"

Henri said, "I'd tell you, Lee, but it's confidential."

She pretended locking her lips, "Not a word."

The old man looked around, then whispered, "I am an agent."

"Ooo . . . a spy? A secret agent?"

"Ha! No, a talent agent and manager for an entertainer."

"Oh, for a singer? A man? A woman? A pisher in the Seine?"

"Not at all, Lee. That was simply an act of nature—But whoa, is this your young man approaching?"

"Why, yes." She waved and called, "Hey, Gerard!"

"*Bonjour*, Lee. *C'est ici!*'"

A young man came over and warmly embraced her.

"Sorry I'm late."

Then seeing the old man, he said, "You seem to be doing okay."

Lee laughed, "Oh, pish, posh." She gave him a gentle nudge.

Nearby a huddled beggar struck up a waltz on his concertina.

Lee held on as Gerard twirled her into a dip.

Tapping his cane, the old man's eyes twinkled.

As the last notes trailed off, Lee tugged Gerard.

"Come. I'd like you to meet someone. Monsieur Henri, this is Gerard."

Gerard searched the old man's features.

" Have we met? At a concert, a music hall?"

"Mnn, I can't say. Maybe the Moulin Rouge today?"

"I don't think so. During the day I write music reviews for newspapers."

Dusk was settling over the declining sun in the west.

"Of course," said Henri. "I think I read your column last night after dinner."

"And was it good?"

"Poached *Saumon*? Yes. But the remains, no. I wrapped them in your paper."

 Gerard stifled, "I meant my column. It was all right?"

"Oh, yes, of course. Very good." Henri opened his pocket watch. "But it grows late. Soon I'll be going to work. Please, would you care to join me for dinner ?"

Lee murmured, "Why, how nice . . ."

As they started across the short Pont St. Louis, Gerard pointed ahead.

"A suggestion, Henri. La Chaussier on the corner. Not the fanciest bistro, but their crab chowder, it is *delicieux*."

Henri said, "Sounds good—and the dessert is up to you."

 "Merci, Henri. I salute your taste—in contrast to the bluenoses who consider me a sniffer of *merde*, rubbish and farts. Ah, but they do pay me handsomely."

"Whaaat? They pay you to trace mankind's garbage?"

"The state pays me, Henri. Public Health. To attend public gatherings and search out polluters and prosecute them."

"More like persecute them," muttered Lee.

"Smokers are prime suspects. Especially with stogies. And coughers, spitters, hackers, sneezers. Drivers who fill the air with fumes, with bacteria. Who litter our streets and contaminate shoppers. Who teach kids and pets to foul our parks and yards."

Lee begged to differ, "Oh, please! I ask, where is your evidence?"

"It surrounds us," waved Gerard. "In the air, our drinking water, our foods, the grass and roadways, insects, trees, pests. Crap everywhere."

"And you trace it? But how?"

"How shall I put it?" he went on. "Do I snoop around with a net? With a nail on a stick? Of course not. Did Dr. Semmelweis? No. He said our beginnings are amid germs, as are our endings. This is especially true, in the reckless waste and orgiastic consumption at the end of the century.

Le fin de siecle we call it. The End of a Century. When every day is a dance, a brouhaha of Whoopee! A cycle of gorging and drinking, and then hurried evacuation— but where? There are no bathrooms, no sewers. Only chamber pots, open kiosks, holes in basements, alleys and the streets! It doesn't look like *L'Age d'Ore*. It doesn't smell like it. It is hardly a golden age at all.

And so we have pollution, disease, we have pestilence, and epidemics, and yea, the plague! Worst of all, we have criminal polluters!

Which is where I come in. But enough about me.. We are on this isle of joy, L'Isle d'St Louis, to enjoy our company. So! . . . time for dessert?"

They had come upon an unpretentious, squat little red brick building, a queue of customers encircling it. As they joined the line, Gerard took a look at the menu posted on the store window.

"Only sorbets tonight: Flavors such as Mango, Papaya, Pomegranate, Watermelon, Avocado, (Eh? Avocado sorbet?) and probably dozens more.

"These are the Berthillon desserts. Not ersatz concoctions by chemists who bombard us with wishful flavors and artificial sweeteners. Here only true liquefactions of the very essence of the fruit will do— that each flavor served shall be true to its origins."

Behind the front counter a poster listed the flavors of the day. As customers mulled over their choices, Gerard noted, "Here one can select exotic peach, pear and apricot flavors. Or from quince to cherry, fig, walnut, or from pink grapefruit, apple, tomato, to all the berries—more than one hundred exquisite flavors.

They were tempted to devour their sorbets. Instead they nipped at them while strolling up the Quai des Gasvries on the right bank to the Pont D'Arcole. Gazing down at the frothing Seine, Henri picked up on his earlier thread.

"Pardon my curiosity, Gerard, and with respect, tell me how do you protect public health?"

Gerard glanced at him, vaguely nettled. "How do you suppose? I look, I sniff, and I wait. For the right sound, the right smell. A sneeze, a cough, some spittle or smoke is a call to action, to arms. And at that point, I move in— Vive la France! I strike! I pounce on the culprit. I seize and arrest him, and turn him over to the gendarmes with my charges.

"And what are the most common charges?

"Well, let me see. A rabid dog, A runaway goat. A cockfight. Rat infestation. Snake raising. Rampant dandruff, allergens, and algae. Food poisoning. Unclean premises. Unquarantined pubs. Tainted water supply. All manner of chemicals, insects, calamities. And many gases—sulphur, propane, methane, many others, even human gas."

At this last, Henri reacted. "No . . . You can't mean— the fart?"

"In France we call it *La Eruption*. One has heard of it, perhaps?"

"Of flatus, yes. The correct word for human gas is Flatus. Remember inflate, deflate."

"Call it flatus or call it fartus. I call it dangerous: On a crowded elevator, also on a Metro train, a dirigible, in church, on a picnic. But for some reason, people make light of it.

At its crude, rupturous sound, people smile. They may tee-hee, and grin, grunt, titter and giggle. Some burst out laughing. But I tell you, at the wrong time and place it can be disastrous. Imagine it occurring during surgery or sex, or at a peace conference, a wedding, a baptism, a courtroom, a funeral, or worse, at an execution.

Lee piped up, "Especially during a guillotine, I'll bet."

Gerard rambled on, "This is when we detectors earn our keep as EM's, attendants, escorts, police, guards and Smell Abaters. Oh, 'tis a most difficult job."

"But what is your training? … your method?"

"My nose. It knows all, smells all. This delicate, sensing, lubricious instrument keeps our air in balance— gases, whiffs, wafts, smoke, smells and scents are grist for its olfactory receptors. It is my acute antenna that I keep at attention, supple and fine-tuned, ready at all times.

"And the perpetrator? Do you always catch him?"

"Ha! Always is an illusion. In truth, no, I do not."

"But a fart? The noise, the odor—an arrest should be easy."

"Nothing of the sort! The kind of crook I seek is a professional of the highest order. A slick operator whose greatest skill is invisibility."

"I believe you will catch him yet. You sound most dedicated, Gerard, and I wish you every success. And now I go to work, at the Elephant Garden. *Allez-vous-en,* my friends!" With a wave they parted and went their ways.

That Evening

"Well, Papa, is this a business? Or a burlesque?"

We were getting dressed for the Elephant Show, practically stumbling over each other to insert our cuff links. No question, this too is part of taking Paris.

"I admit it, I was skeptical. But now I do believe we have found our market. Our tour in Lyon opened my eyes. In our first few weeks I saw dozens, perhaps hundreds of people paying for repeat shows."

"Indeed, Papa, and we have seen much more than 6,000 francs!" I jiggled the money bag. But I could tell. Papa still had his doubts.

"Of all the gases, tell me Jean, which is the worst?"

"Worst? None. But if you mean stinkiest, I'd have to say hydrogen is the most potent. You know that awful "rotten egg" stink? That's good old hydrogen sulfide at its worst, a leader in extra-uncomfortable, odoriferous vapors. Less stinky are nitrogen and oxygen.

But none are like plain air. Inhale too much, gulp down food too quickly, sigh frequently, and snore a lot in your sleep . . . and, like it or not, you are building a bomb.

We know that certain foods can also improve on farts. Will they be weasels? Or will they be thunderbolts? They come down to various proteins, sugars, and fats as they break down in the intestines.

The common trouble-makers are broccoli, Brussels sprouts, onions, garlic, peanuts, cauliflower, cabbage, radishes, apples, chili, fast foods, and fried foods, Then there are nuts, raisins, berries, also coffee, colas, pizza, spaghetti, salad, fish, hot dogs, alcohol, beer, spices, licorice, tomatoes, beans, chickpeas, lentils, milk, yogurt, cheese, eggs, bran, and cucumbers. All terrific exploders."

And let us not forget their partners— potent cooking methods like frying, searing, broiling, braising and grilling. And how about smoking and stewing, sautéing and pickling? A cooking method can go a long way to exploit them.

Studying these has led me into further fart facts:

- It takes ten minutes for swallowed food to get to the large intestine.

- The average person releases 14 farts/day; that's 98 farts per week!

- Delayed farts can be seen as dark cloudy masses in X-rays.

- Then there are many start-up farts that try to exit but fizzle out.

- Swimming, singing, snoring also ingest large quantities of air.

- My point here is that one should not delay evacuating the intestines.

- Wrestling and prize fights have strict rules against farting.

- Fights have actually been called due to fighter asphyxiation.

- Morticians once massaged the departed to evacuate residual gases.

- At the Crusades voiding wind was rated a Saracen offense.

- In China, Taoism forbids farting in a northerly direction.

- Early French hookers once paid a toll of one fart to cross Montcluc Bridge.

- This led to excessive toll fees, increased traffic and some drownings.

"And so, Papa, your first task will be publicity. You will build contacts in the media, while I will gain us notice in the news media. How? By alerting the public to a mysterious wave of gross indiscretions. If this be *Le Fin de Siecle*, I will re-christen it *La Fart de Siecle.* "

That afternoon a series of complaints were lodged with police departments and the Surete by upset store managers. At first they were irregular. A call for airing out a Fauchon store and a bus. Then a woman reported a vulgar noise in the Musee D'Orsay. That a certain nude Rodin statue had actually tooted.

Before this could be confirmed, an officer said his K-9 police dog had gone berserk and traced a suspect's trail of staccato farts. It led the officer to a Boy Scout troop.

Then there was a frantic child at the Parc de La Villette who threw up in the Hippo restaurant fearing what he thought were gaseous hippos.

A dentist in La Defense was distressed by a patient's gas as he was giving her gas.

At the bird stalls near Notre Dame, the canaries were asphyxiated by noxious fumes.

The manager of the Comedie Francaise complained his theatre was being smothered in farts.

Several calls to the police reported domestic family duels involved farting.

Metro riders actually tried to open windows to rid their train of traveling farts.

Men peeing in the waterfall at the Bois de Boulogne. One guy farted, all got mad and shoved an innocent lawyer into the pool. He is suing the Bois.

The bundled cat and dog at Galleries Lafayette were separated when they blew at each other.

Onlookers of Mona Lisa's portrait in the Louvre complained of its rotten egg odor. Some one had sprayed the painting with hydrogen.

At the Pere La Chaise cemetery women lined up to stroke Oscar Wilde's memorial organ. They wanted to hear it beep.

On and on they came, from all levels of citizenry, young and old. A flood of nasty complaints. Was there a gas leak somewhere?

Arriving at the Reservations Desk for the Elephant Garden, we were passed through with a troupe of musicians reporting for work. Immaculately attired in impeccable taste, we two gentlemen were shown to a small side table, our capes covering our theatrical costumes.

Here we beheld a mock jungle—a fantasmagoria of exotic palms, surging waterfalls, erupting volcanoes. Here and there, giant snakes slithered through trees, baboons swung overhead, elegant ladies rode white stallions bareback, and menacing aborigines confronted suave guests. Bristling over this tropical tangle stood a thirty-foot warrior elephant, clearly a *papier mache* mastodon.

It immediately reminded us of the hollow Greek wooden horse filled with armed soldiers. This mastodon had huge rheumy melancholic eyes and an enlarged trunk used for trumpeting wild cheers or displeasure. We were so impressed by the ersatz elephant that we moved to a closer table. Here we heard its internal rumblings—men drinking, cursing, bantering, and so on. We could even hear instructions given to pan the new Gassoon act.

At this, Papa was ready to dismember the elephant. But I cautioned him, "Let us make this a successful debut." And I waited backstage for my introduction.

During the wait, Papa scanned the guests; yes, his editors were here. This could be a momentous debut. Finally, with a tympani roll and a cymbal smash, the moment came.

The master of ceremonies stepped forth to present a new performer at the Elephant Garden of Le Moulin Rouge. He knew my name, but that was all. Yet he introduced me as the "hottest thing since *crepes suzette*. Please give your kind attention to . . . Monsieur Gassoon!"

I gingerly stepped into the spotlight and smiled. Ever the gentleman, I held a pair of white gloves and wore my long sweeping mantle.

I advanced to stage center, and began my curtain raiser.

"I ask you, is there any sound more stirring, more poignant than a baby's cry? (DOES CRYING BABY EFFECTS.) The source shocks the audience.

"And at the beach is there anything more urgent than a swimmer calling for rescue? (DOES WATER EFFECTS, CLANGING BUOY, ENDING WITH CRY.) Audience is now stirred.

"And for sheer distress, consider the shepherd tending his flock when it is suddenly approached by wolves. (PANICKED SHEEP, THEN RAVENOUS WOLVES, FINALLY A SINGLE WARNING HORN.) Audience cries out, pointing to my rear.

"Could you 'see' these situations? Of course! And so you see how real sounds can be, and how capable we are to sense any sound, some soft and intimate, other sounds as loud and pressing as . . .well, as this. (LONELY, ECHOING FART). Audience applauds, at last understanding my act.

"And so, to me, sounds are my passion and my bread and butter. But enough of such disasters. How much better when we join in a song of hope and faith. A song we all know as "Brother John." Your attention, please. While I affix this tiny harmonica in my rear . . ."

I sang the first line "*Frere Jacque, Frere Jacque,*"

But for the last "*Jacque,*" my butt tooted on the harmonica,

And I held my hand to my ear thrilled with the note.

I did the same with "*Dorme Vous, Dorme Vous.*"

The song kept on for five more verses. And so did I in the same style, conspicuously switching the instruments in my bum—kazoo, ocarina, flute, slide-whistle, and finally, as a crowning touch, bagpipes. Each blew one note, satisfying the crowd that these were indeed wind-actuated, and that my butt provided the only sound and tonal variation.

"Imagine that!{" I could hear from the front rows.

"Some one actually putting his arse into a useful art!"

When I tooted the final "Dong" they were charmed, and fully captivated.

Some sat bolt upright and roared. While others stood, some leaned forward the better to hear. But all reacted with childish glee, and all sang along.

I believe I could have performed a *symphonette* and won their approval.

Finally, they thundered Bravo! Demanding an encore. But it was clear I was pretty well aerated. I thanked them and took several musical bows well in tune with familiar songs. Some clapped along, and many hummed along. It was clear this one small children's song was the hit of the evening. And how went the Elephant? To the band's musical curtain it did a cheery buck and wing. Upon the closing note, the audience applauded wildly.

Back in my dressing room, a visitor was waiting, the boss himself.

"*Bonsoir*, Monsieur Oller. What a pleasant surprise. I see you've met my agent and manager, Monsieur Jetsam." I said, referring to Papa who sat there shrugging, looking befuddled. "Yes, yes, we've been discussing a schedule for next month. I hope you don't mind."

"Mind? Let me tell you what I do mind. That your schedule is for one month. Next month? I'm sure we can do better."

"Then tell me," Oller asked. "What terms would you prefer?

"The same ones that other headliners have," I said.

Monsieur Oller leaned back, and delivered a lecture.

"Our stars are time-tested with our audiences. They virtually guarantee a predictable attendance. None of them performs crudities. Not a one endangers the prestige of my nightclub or can get me sued or worse yet, closed down."

I lit a cigarette and sighed. This was going to be a while. "Of course, Monsieur Oller. I understand. And we are prepared to insure against such risks. But you ask what we have in mind? Only what's fair:

- A one-year contract with renewal options for three more years.
- A signing bonus, and increases based on attendance growth.
- Featured billing and ongoing media advertising and publicity.
- Annual promotional budget for hiring four support ladies."

Oller was changing color, "And that's it? That's all? Why not ask for the goddam Elephant while you're at it? And our Wine Cellars with our 9,000 liters of prize-winning champagnes? Gassoon, you ask for the moon!"

"Yes, it costs," I said dryly. "Good work always does, and it is worth it. Look around Paris, and you know what it takes to succeed among today's dog-eat-dog nightclubs. You must outdo the rest. And overcome jaded appetites. And you must outdo with top-grade talents, comforts and pleasures. To make more, you must spend more. And here is my guarantee: Exciting shows. Big audiences. Big spenders. And steadily growing business. Think it over. And tomorrow let's go over the contract."

I held the door open. "Thank you, Monsieur Oller, and *bonsoir*."

He seemed to be mumbling to himself under his breath as he put on his homburg and great fur coat, and shuffled out. He paused, turning to air another point.

But having had my say, I firmly closed the door.

I turned to Pop and waggled my eyebrows, "Well?"

He fanned himself and barely audibly uttered. "Whoosh . . ."

I continued, "I had to straighten him out, tonight or never. So I did, Papa. Tomorrow he'll come through, you'll see. Maybe not the whole menu, but ample enough for now. You'll see."

"If you say so, Jean. But you know, you were excellent in the Garden tonight. Almost tossed you a few francs myself!"

Our media friends were also delighted, as reflected in their morning papers:

"A daring new comic has come to town."

"Monsieur Gassoon is here; An antic name you won't forget."

"New at Moulin Rouge! An Impertinent Star!"

On and on it went, and many of its nuances were presented and discussed on radio talk shows.

We didn't lose any sleep listening to it on the hotel radio.

We had heard all the dazzling *encomiums* before, in Marseille, in Lyon. Instead we dined on an excellent late dinner and headed straight to bed, our ears ringing with echoes of applause and encores. We slept blissfully and then after a hearty breakfast, curled up around our suite reading sections of Paris newspapers, occasionally reading an excerpt aloud.

Pariscope wrote this— "Imagine a new comedy sensation! Imagine a sound effects clown with nausea, stomach trouble, gas! Then see him at le Moulin Rouge. His name is Monsieur Gassoon (*quelle a nomer*!) Last night he gave a Paris premiere at the exotic Elephant Gardens of the Moulin Rouge to end all premieres. And the Boulevard de Clichy is still laughing!"

We read this, too, in the Gazette—

"Monsieur Gassoon presented himself as a virtual concert performer elegantly attired in high style— red silk breeches, brocade gold vest, black embroidered tails, and so on, every garment designed for dramatic effect. He then proceeded to lambaste his illusion to high heaven. For he went on to destroy traditions we hold dear: Lullabys, dating and mating, military maneuvers, love songs. All were vanquished by a flip of his hip and rowdy explosive sound effects alone . . ."

"And get this review, Pop, in the Observatoire—

"One high society matron was heard to observe, 'If the *Fin de Siecle* is not over yet, this outgoing young man has just driven a nail into it and buried it for all time. Last night Monsieur Gassoon came in with the rain, and left on a high note. One might almost say, left in a flurry! "

We were both having a good laugh when we heard the doorbell. Papa pleasantly opened it to admit our prospective boss, Monsieur Oller. Under his arm he carried the same periodicals we had been reading, his fingers drumming (or trembling?) on them. He grumbled as if trying to say hello. Then seeing our spread of news sections, he simply dumped his stack on the floor. "Huh! Apparently all of Paris salutes you!"

I casually said, "Yes, it is nice, Charles. (Now by first name.) Have a seat. Some coffee?" My good manners seemed to calm him, and Papa helped him off with his coat and hat.

Monsieur Oller paused in his deep breathing to look around for an ash tray. I brought him one.

Immediately Oller aired his rants, "My staff, my people are having fits! Who released this publicity? Who permitted it? Who wrote it? This simply won't do. Our current stars are demanding redress, equal space and praise. Even the Divine Sarah is up in arms!"

"*Quel domage,*" I agreed. "A pity. But while we are not in your hire, we do tend to act independently as regards media, and frankly we've found it doesn't shrink revenues one iota. Matter of fact, you will see tonight that it generally attracts more business."

Oller could only growl, "We'll see, we shall see . . . My main reason for this visit is to invite you to join our company. Once an audience gets comfortable with your kind of act, we believe we can shape it into a first class hit."

"Really? You would do that? And we would allow it? Monsieur, please. We are not rank amateurs. We are already professionals. One -of -a-kind. Shaped by daily contact with our audiences, and familiar with them for the past six years. And if there's anything we know better than anyone, it is making audiences feel comfortable with us. I am so glad you came today. And that you'd like to add us to your great organization. It gives us a chance to discuss mutual terms."

"Terms? (A sudden coughing spell almost gagged him.) Ah yes, the terms. I've gone over the four points discussed last night and while I find some difficult and iffy, I'd say we are within range.

1) Re your one-year contract with options for three more years. Mmmm, yes.

2) Re a signing bonus, and increases based on attendance growth. Not quite possible now, needs a baseline and comparative attendance figures.

3) Re featured billing, no. It impinges on other stars. But support in media, yes.

4) Re budget for annual promotional staff such as hiring four support aides. Not now.

This will require a renewable itemized proposal each year."

Pop and I sat back thinking it over. Not bad for a start. We had agreement on three out of four points. I offered my hand to Oller and thanked him for his preparation, and said we needed to review this on our own. We'd come by later this afternoon.

We had a thoughtful, peaceful lunch, each of us meditating over Oller's rebuttal. Then, over coffee and an éclair, our opinions tumbled out. Pop went first. "Sounds good to me. Fair, reasonable, a working plan we can build on."

"Have to agree, though I did hold my breath; I only expected one for four. But the real goldmine will begin with year two. That's when these terms get updated and we hit our stride. But for now let's go ahead as is. Maybe we'll walk over to the Rouge and sign the papers."

"Maybe my ass. I'll race you, Junior," he added, "And beat you by two yards!"

Monsiur Oller arched one eyebrow at our barging in that afternoon.

But he replaced his monocle and flashed his hidden smile. He was gap-toothed. "Ah, welcome, my new *attraits*! Come in.

"Feel free to visit any time, and mix and mingle with our other stars. The next few days will be busy as we prepare for your opening night. I think it can be this Saturday night."

I gulped. In three days?

"Assuming you know your every detail, every nuance of your act, we have people here to make sure you enjoy a big success— people to make your display photographs. Music people for fanfares, underscores, climax points that integrate with our orchestra. Wardrobe and makeup people to enhance your appearance.   And of course, ad agencies and publicity people to get word around.

Can all of this be done in three days? Of course not.

But we can start and schedule it. So I'm assigning you a connection to our service pool, a young lady who will serve as your secretary. We want to keep you well apprised and well organized because we'd like you with us for a good long time."

"Thank you," I said. "We'd like that, too. Starting today. Shall we now sign the contract ?"

"Yes, yes," said Oller, reaching for a folder headed "Gassoon."

It looked like the Magna Carta. I handed it to Pop to digest. Oller waited with his pen.

"And there's this, Monsieur Oller. Ahem, the matter of salary. When you planned all this, what salary did you have in mind?"

It was Oller's turn to gulp. "In mind? Like what can we afford? It strikes me that with the start-up expenses, the best that we can offer is 6,000 francs."

"6,000 per month?"

I took the Gassoon folder from Pop, and neatly replaced it on Oller's desk.

"Regrettably, we must decline it."

Wearily, I clarified our position. "In Marseille, perhaps. But we turned down 6,000 per month in Lyon. Which is what brought us to Paris. And now we are prepared to produce and perform the only truly unique act in all of Paris . . ."

"Yes? For how much?"

"Our price is 8,000 francs per month. Complete."

Oller's eyes rolled, then stared evenly at me.

I didn't blink, neither did he. He reached for the folder, turned to the last page, and did some hurried scratching. He then slammed the whole folder back on the desk.

"Nah! All right?"

I opened it and saw he had written in 8,000 francs/ mo.

"Oui, de rien. Done and done." I signed the contract, and asked him to initial his change. When he did, I asked for a copy, and one thing more.

Oller hung his head and mumbled, 'What ? What more?"

I was clear: "I realize the signing bonus has been deferred, and we accept that for now. But."

Oller grumbled, "Well, what?"

"We will need some sort of advance. What show people call "walking around" money."

"What? You can't walk?"

"Petty cash for cigarettes, coffee, you know."

"How much walking?"

I thought, "Oh, about 3,000 francs. Each."

Mechanically, Oller reached into a pocket and pulled out a roll of currency. Barely seeing it, he pulled out six big notes, "Walk, walk . . ." and handed them to me.

I split them with Pop, and with a quick *merci* to Oller, we beat a hasty *Bon Jour* out the door.

Second things second: Lodging. Our little fleabag hotel would never do as suitable quarters for two rising *bon vivants*.

Several alternates came to mind—the Cracker Barrel down in Montparnasse, the Empire Duster off rue Frederick Sauton near Boulevard St. Germain. Then there was the Place des Vosges in the Marais, an elegant and expensive square far beyond our present means.

But the one we fancied was the odd-shaped Bateau-Lavoir in Montmartre. Located on the back street of Rue Garreau, it looked like a rundown barge and laundry, but it did have its advantages.

A short walk to St. Germain, the cultural heart of town, and a one-stop Metro ride to Place Pigalle and the Rouge. It was also near a famous art colony, La Place du Tertre, a favorite hangout of portraitists, art dabblers and dilettantes.

Above all, it was a great crossroads for friends and artists. Here there was no shortage of kindred souls. Granted that they came and went, and were a vain and fickle lot, still such minds illuminated and cheered a dreary day.

Here one could bandy words with the charm and wit of Apollinaire, Max Jacob, Zola on various days. Among the painters was the little firebrand Toulouse-Lautrec; there was Cezanne. Monet. Utrillo. For music we had Offenbach and Hoffman. All surrounded by a fawning corps de ballet, and musicians. We could ask for nothing more, and so we rented a suite.

After rejuvenating showers, we sat about with schnapps and cigars and took stock.

"Well, Pop, did we make it as planned?" I began.

Thoughtfully, he stirred his Holland gin with his pinkie. "Well it'sh better than baking."

"Yes, Pop, we've had quite a time. And I realize your trial month is winding down soon. But we are definitely ahead. On the brink, in fact, of exploding this so-called goldmine of mine.

"So what do you think?

"Do you want to collect your share now and zip back to your biscuits and baguettes? Or . . . are you ready to sign on with Gassoon, in this courageous venture and take home a shitpile of gold? Well?"

Slightly pie-eyed, Pop grinned, "What do you tink I tink? That I would let you get me all *saoueler*? That I would let you get the pay-off and I'd get the crumbs? Hell no! Remember who makes the dough. The baker! And who's the best in Provence? Me! You damn right that time. And I'm staying, I'll see this through and get half. We're partners, all right!"

"I covered his hand with mine. "Partners for sure."

Pop rested his hand over mine, "And don't you forget it."

Here at the Bateau, life is as one always wished it would rather be. No noise, no drunks. No smells or kiddies. One could read or write or paint to your heart's content, and converse at ease, quietly, thoughtfully. Pop and I could stuff our pipes, tamp them a tiddle, and get back in touch with ourselves. If we only had a match.

"Pop," I said, "I wonder. Do you have an old-fashioned wooden kitchen match?"

He fished through his pockets. "Sorry. But sit tight. I'll go downstairs and get one." In minutes he was back, bringing with him a studious young man.

Pop handed me a match, and introduced him. "Say hello to Gerard, a free-lance writer and a Board of Health free thinker. And get this, he writes theatre reviews for some of the newspapers."

"*Merveilleux!* A pleasure to meet you, Gerard."

"And you, too. Monsieur Henri has told me so much about your act."

"I'm sure, since he is my partner as well as my agent, manager, and father. And I do look forward to working with you."

Pop beamed from ear to ear, "You know, Gerard, we have just arrived from Lyon. And we definitely need some one to show us around. Are you interested in the job?"

"Of course, if I was younger and not so tied up as I am. But I thank you for the kind offer. And maybe I do know someone. An art student, well educated and responsible. You met her, Henri—yesterday, at L'Isle de St. Louis. Remember?

"Yes, yes. Lee. Of course. She'd be perfect."

Gerard said, "I'm seeing her for lunch. And if you like, I can mention the subject and send her to you. Say about 2 p.m."

"Excellent. We can both interview her. And we thank you for your help."

Promptly at two, pert little Lee was at our door. A light knock-knock, and we welcomed her. Granted ours were not the showiest show business quarters, still we conveyed a formal atmosphere, firm and reliable, which bodes for a good beginning.

"Ah, Lee. *Bonjour* and come in," Henri took her hand.

He offered her a comfortable armchair, and introduced her to me.

"Please. I'd like you to meet the head of our company. This is Monsieur

Gassoon, the newest entertainer signed on at Le Moulin Rouge. His first name is Jean."

"Good to see you both. My friend Gerard said you may have a part-time job for me. Part-time because I am a full-time student at L'Ecole des Beaux Arts."

"Yes," I agreed. "Gerard is correct. And I will tell you what it is. I do a frank comedy routine at the Rouge. Frank because it seems to affect some women in an emotional way. They just laugh themselves silly or keel over, and once in awhile, cry. At that point, they generally need some friendly care. Perhaps a hankie, a cold towel, maybe some smelling salts or ice water, and some rest. Certainly, any upset person needs a care-giver. Would you like to be one?"

Lee was thinking it over. "Gosh, I don't know. A few questions. What bothers these people? Exactly what do you do that's so upsetting?"

She had gotten right to the nub of it—asking the pointed question.

I must have gulped twice, and then said, "Well, for entertainment's sake, I fart."

She burst a laugh, "You—what? You fart? And then what?"

"Then that's all. But I do it in such a clever, elegant way, people applaud."

She shook her head. "They must be *pazzo*. Nuts. They pay to be farted at. And get what, a Raspberry? A Bronx cheer? A pee-yew?"

"Huh? You call it that in America?"

"Oh much more. I even heard it called the Gas Lax, and get this, the Dry Shits!"

"No, really? How gauche. How dare they?"

"I'll tell you all about it. But first tell me about the job. Will this be from eight to midnight, every night? Will it include any matinées?"

I could tell she was interested. She found it amusing

"Yes, Lee. Eight to twelve, and it will include two matinées a week."

She went on, "A care-giver sounds like first aid. Will I need a nursing license?"

My answer, "I don't think so. You'll be serving as an attendant or usherette."

Another question: "Will I be the only care-giver? Who else will be on duty?"

Pop's answer: "You will be part of a staff of four at each performance."

Lee asked, "Are we required to wear white? Who will provide this?"

I answered, "Yes, though not necessarily uniforms. We will provide each of you with white jackets."

She asked, " How much will we be paid, and when?"

My answer, "You will get ten francs per upset patron plus ten francs more per caring hour. Every Friday. Now how do you feel about joining up with us?

Lee stuck her hand out. Each of us gave it a shake and we were set.

We'd all rehearse on Friday, and go to work Saturday. No sooner did she skip downstairs than I glanced at my neighbor's newspaper.

There on the front page were three faces, Nederland, Entwhistle, and Glomerulke. A rogues gallery of the cronies of the Donor Organ Gang. Looking like grave diggers, they had a knack of dickering for donated body parts before they were donated. At one time they actually had their eye on me.

The next two days were a blur. An orange and blue streak of nonstop getting things done. Chasing around for hand props, show props, gifts. More interviews. More chasing for paint, dressing room accessories like phones, lamps and bulbs. Medical accessories from thermometers to a wheel chair, stretchers, A gurney table, sheets and pillows, blankets, crutches, canes, a walker, stretchers, a wheelchair.

Then came clothing—two complete dress suits with shirts, stockings, shoes. Four white outfits for attendants, size M, including white shoes, stockings, medical jackets and caps. What more? Complete office supplies and record books. All to be delivered to our Moulin Rouge dressing room no later than Saturday.

All Friday was devoted to training Lee and her attendants. Part of this included rehearsals of the act and each girl taking notes as dictated by Papa and I.

What became especially important was the use of code phrases to gain their attention and signal certain duties. In some cases, a patron may faint, lose self-control or get hysterical. In these conditions there are three alternative steps to take:

Resuscitate: Fan the patron, offer water or give air or smelling salts. If patron is male, Papa will attend to him.

Let Her Rest: Leave her as is and add a pillow, cool towel or ice.

Move Her Carefully: Use stretcher or wheelchair to get patron out of the hall.

Take patron to a designated backstage ICU for a nap and a signed release form.

During rehearsals, a senior musician worked up a cue sheet for musical punctuations—fanfares, stingers, suspense bridges, emphases, crescendos, intros, and wrap-ups. These he practiced during key portions of our rehearsing. Soon our entire ensemble was ready for a dress rehearsal by Friday eve. And so as to memorize all cues, we did several rehearsals.

The next day was confirmed as our Opening Night. It was announced throughout print and radio media. As an extra touch it was also newscast from the transmitter atop the new Eiffel Tower. By Saturday noon there was hardly a man, woman or child in Paris who had not heard of Monsieur Gassoon. The slang said "the gas man is coming" to the Moulin Rouge tonight. Because nothing circulates better than rumor and innuendo, we accompanied our bland public announcements with a suggestive whispering campaign.

"They say he can fire off farts at will." "Oh yeah? Who's Will?"

"I heard his farts are all a vocal trick, that he's really a ventriloquist!"

"He's a walking fart machine, and he can trash the Metro. Ohmigod!"

"This I've got to see and hear!" "And don't worry about smell. There is none."

"A fake? Just light a match at his butt. But not too close!"

By noon the Gassoon premiere was sold out at 20,000 francs. Now began an accelerating rush for scalper's tickets. Box seats that had been 350 francs began to climb to 700 and 1,000 francs, and champagne liters went at matching prices. Soon the Moulin Rouge was offering SRO tickets—Standing Room Only for 200 francs—and doing a land office business.

That night Pop and I had a royal dinner. Feeling we were either about to put on our best show or possibly be run out of town, we dined at the most swank, lavish restaurant we knew. It was Le Grande Vefour on the rue de Beaujolaix, facing the Tuilleries Gardens. Considered one of the most attractive restaurants in all Paris, it was a renowned favorite of Napoleon and Josephine. What did we order and have? Only the best of everything, enough to assure us a good night's rest. And sleep soundly we did.

Considering this was our Big Day, Saturday seemed to come at full gallop, leaving little time for the niceties of a leisurely breakfast. Instead we had the Parisian's classic fare: coffee and a *brioche* with sharp cheese, and we were off to a meeting with M. Oller and his staff.

It turned out that all parties were prepared. Everything was on hand; everybody was ready for what appeared to be another glorious page in Moulin Rouge history.

Warmth and bonhomie cheer circled our crew, setting the scene for our morning run-through. With its secrets and labyrinthine corridors, the backstage area harbors a thousand and one treasures. We met the expert artisans who will unveil the recipe for excellence which has made the Moulin Rouge famous.

We saw numerous talents at work in this timeless enclave which knew neither night nor day nor the passage of time. These are costumers and tailors, carpenters and set designers, electricians and lighting engineers, artisans whose efforts are unified in a common goal.

The secret ateliers of the Moulin Rouge were unveiled. We visited the well-guarded sumptuous wardrobes of the legendary Miss Doriss Girls dancers; met our musical chef; toured the vast collection of lingerie and feather arrangers, watched master bootmakers.

As is customary, our rehearsals were not detailed. We only presented highlights, cues, turning points, and props. Words, jokes, slight moves would be rehearsed later. Curtains, sets, lighting changes, sound control, and smooth flow were the major concerns of the stage manager, and his staffers, all of whom took profuse notes. Overseeing each element and the overall rhythm of the show, M. Oller dictated numerous notes to his secretaries.

Meanwhile, Henri and I familiarized ourselves with backstage protocol, the Who's Who, and do's and don'ts. My dressing room was large and well furnished with ample armchairs and couches, even a comfortable twin bed for napping. A nap? The best idea yet.

It is early, 4 p.m. I have several hours for rehearsal and leisure before curtain time. My stage clothes and props are carefully organized, my makeup well laid out. I note that I have excellent stage access without imminent traffic jams or nearby crowds.

My opening night, the biggest night of my career—at the Moulin Rouge, and I had napped for two hours! Where was my makeup, props, my costume and staff?

I collected Papa, gave him a timing sheet and prop list, and we went over the timing list. We could see that the entire show was structured to run in six twenty-minute segments, a total of two hours.

How did it go? How was that first might at the Moulin Rouge? Better than expected. Of course, being in the center of it was like being in the eye of the hurricane; it all spun in and around my senses. For an accurate view I had to refer to the next day's reviews. The major review was by Gerard Deladier.

Moulin Rouge Does it Again! Surprise Hit of the Year! Monsieur Gassoon Premiere All the Rage

by Gerard Deladier

Yesterday Monsieur Gassoon was another Paris clown. Unknown. Unnoticed. And unfunny. But in one night, after one performance at Le Moulin Rouge he became a Star. Such was the comic magnitude of the Great Gassoon, a talent not seen in Paris in many years.

What was the show like? What did this upstart comic do? Some might say he did vocal impressions. Did speech imitations. That he did animal voices. Sounds of machinery and weaponry. That he could imitate musical instruments. Underwater creatures. But the incredible feature of his sounds is that all were emanating from his derriere!

One might suppose that he committed a vulgar act, gaseous and odorous. But au contraire, he performed in good taste, producing no gas and absolutely no malodorous vapors.

Further excellence was in Gassoon's care to costume design. He presented himself in high fashion elegance: a black satin tuxedo jacket with tails, red satin breeches to the knees, white rib-knit hosiery, Richelieu patent leather pumps with gold-tone buckles, a blousy white poet's shirt, floppy white butterfly bow tie, a gold brocade vest, and a pair of white gloves held in his hand.

A Rare Sales Record

Monsieur Gassoon led the grand parade of talent that opened the show. His primo act preceded Chevalier, Piaff, Bernhart, and Mistinguette,and at 20,000 francs average income per patron, it outdid all previous attendance income for premieres. And it was the only act that received a nonstop flood of applause resulting in eleven curtain calls. His popularity may be further measured by the evening's renewed reservations for future shows.

It is customary and understandable in a respectful review such as this to salute a newly discovered talent by honoring it with a special commendation in the world's legendary Hall of Performing Arts, a place somewhat above the first rank. I am honored to designate that place for Monsieur Gassoon.

A Dance Without Drawers?

Of course, as usual the cancan proved to be the highpoint of the evening. Where did the cancan come from? According to my *Oxford Companion to Music*, it has defined the cancan as "A boisterous and slatternly dance of the quadrille order, exact origin unknown."

It may have come from working-class dance halls where drawers were unknown. These appeared in the 1850s with the advent of hoop skirts and crinolines.

The first drawers were essentially two tubes of material, one for each leg, and none for the crotch. This is perhaps the source. But Le Moulin Rouge does not permit such revealing garments.

In Paris in the 19th century, the French cancan was born—a highly choreographed quadrille offering dancers the opportunity to display their limbs.

The main moves are the high kick or *battement*, the *rond de jambe* (quick rotary movement of lower leg with knee raised and skirt held up), the *port d'armes* (turning on one leg, while grasping the other leg by the ankle and holding it almost vertical), the cartwheel and the *grand écart* (the flying or jump splits). It is *de rigueur* for dancers to yelp.

The cancan later became viewed as erotic when the dancers displayed extravagant underwear, and black fishnet stockings. They lifted their skirts much more, and used a move considered cheeky and provocative—bending over and throwing their skirts over their backs, presenting their bottoms to the audience. The Moulin Rouge prima donna La Goulue is well known for this, and embroidered a heart on the seat of her drawers.

*   *   *

The girls came spilling out in a dream routine, all attired in flowing Grecian gowns.

The classic themed music then struck a fast Belle-Epoque beat and the dancers almost ignited, whirling off their lofty robes to reveal far more earthy dresses. These they swirled into a joyous, squealing corps of can-can dancers. It was a gay, exciting circle that brought on La Goulue to introduce tonight's prima ballerina, the American jazz guest dancer Josephine Baker. Wearing a girdle of ripe bananas and little else, she pivoted her way around the floor attracting cheers, huzzahs, and applause. At last, when she had distributed all her bananas, she spun off —to bring on the evening's surprise performer.

It was my cue to adroitly enter from stage left. I came on holding a single lit candle.

I advanced to stage center and peered through a dozen spots and floods. After a lengthy pause, I spoke. "I am looking for an honest man. Any volunteers? Never mind, tonight I will light the way to a new form of Belle-Epoque entertainment."

I strolled to a far corner, which had a small table. I put the candle in a holder, all the while continuing my patter. "You cannot see it, feel it or touch it, but it is quite real. How real? (BLOWS FART) Oops, *excuse-moi*. This entertainment is so new it's blowing in the wind; and I invite your interest." By now I was back at stage center and bowed to each side, "*Bienvenu*, honorable *mesdames et monsieurs*. It is a distinct pleasure to greet you on this occasion, my debut at the beautiful Moulin Rouge. I am Jean Vent-Jean, known as Monsieur Gassoon. And I am here to light your way to a new entertainment."

With that, I whirled off my cape and let the audience take in my outlandish outfit. Their eyes boggled. It was so bizarre that it evoked a laugh, telling viewers this was to be a comic turn. They whispered to each other. They were curious. I continued. "On that note, shall we get into a friendly mood with a little song.

How about "*Frere Jacque?*"

I raised my arm to begin a down beat, when—

"Oops. Dropped my glove. *Excusez-moi.*"

I bent to retrieve it, and blew a mighty boomer. The audience really didn't know how to react. Suspicion? Shock? Offended? Curious? Giggly?

I begged their pardon, "Sorry. Now we sing —

My other arm went up, and the other glove fell! I shook my head and smiled weakly,

"*Je regrette.* I get these palpitations"...

Reaching down for the glove I launched a blast. This time they caught on. It was a stunt! It was all a stunt from a farting clown. They gasped, they roared! How daring! I held up a tiny harmonica, then poked it in my butt.

"This will soothe the savage beast. Yes, I've stuck it you know, where the sun doesn't shine.

And now, "*Frere Jacque.*" All together, *s'il vous plait.*"

I sang the first line "*Frere Jacque, Fre-re* . . .TOOT!" But for the word "*Jacque*" I tooted the harmonica. What harmonica? None was visible. Holding my hand to my ear as if enraptured, I did the same with "Dorme Vous, Dorme . . . TOOT!"

The song goes on for five more verses. And so did I, inserting alternate instruments in my *derriere*—kazoo, ocarina, flute, slide-whistle, and finally, the bagpipes. Each gust aired a beautiful note. Each blew one clear note affirming its source

When I had piped the song's final "Dong" they were charmed. This was not crude; it was an amusing novelty. Some sat bolt upright and roared. Some craned, thrilled. And others stood, leaning forward all the better to hear. But all reacted with glee. I believe I could have easily performed a symphony.

At last, they thundered Bravo, demanding an encore. By this time I was relaxed enough for a cigarette. I showed them a thin rubber tubing. I then inserted it in my anus and lit a cigarette. After I did so, I slowly inhaled my cigarette. In a few seconds I exhaled the smoke from the tube. It floated out as a perfectly formed smoke ring!

The audience's jaws sagged in utter disbelief, and then the applause began. Not the spontaneous sort, but insistent rhythmic clapping that demands a repeat.

So I did a few rings, and as a *finale* a holiday wreath. Then I offered a gift for the kiddies at home.

"Mustn't forget the little angels and bring home a little memento, something pretty …"

In quick succession I inflated six toy balloons, tied them and batted them to the audience.

It was now time to wrap up with my peak number—my imitations of women's voices "as you've never heard them." And I went into the sound effects of the maiden, the newlywed, honeymooner, mother-in-law and the harridan. But I added a slight extra touch. At each TOOT, I seemed to be bumped forward a step, putting a comic cap on a rather uncouth act. They laughed, they loved it.

This not only got belly laughs, it practically brought down the house. It certainly kept the Swooner Girls busy.

To cries of "Encore!" and the rolling rhythm of the orchestra I went on to do several encores, starting with the sounds of youngsters at potty training, all the way to old-timers fighting constipation. This became my longest-running routine and I felt I had done my assigned stint.

Time to wrap up. A closing song should do it. Perhaps "Toot Toot Tootsie, *Touché*"? No, too obvious. Better end with something sweet …

"By now you may think you've heard it all, and perhaps so. But there is still my *coup de couronne*, my crowning stroke. For those of you who enjoy the lovely "Clair de Lune," you will remember this version for many years. Patience please, and *c'est la!*"

I brushed aside a coat tail and from under my arm I brought forth a small, elegant gold-polished soprano saxophone. In one fluid motion I affixed it to my bottom, placed my hands on the keys behind my back and tooted the plaintive melody. The tune was simple, clear and mellifluous. While I could only sustain the first four bars, that's all it took to bring applause. "Incredible!" came the outcries. "Amazing!" "Brilliant!" came from ladies weeping tears of joy.

I was about to thank the crowd and beg off when, whoops—hadn't I forgotten the candle on the corner table? Cautioning the audience for silence, I approached the candle and studied it. I measured its distance to my backside and implored the heavens. Methodically, I grunted once, and from a distance of two feet, TOOT, my butt blew out the flame.

So much for sleight of rectum. A gushing burst of applause, and that clinched my show. I left to a series of curtain call bows.

Back in my dressing room Papa and Gerard were toasting each other. I collapsed on the couch, my hand begging for a small whiskey. Flattering comments were unnecessary. We all knew we had set Paris on its ass.

One sip, and a glance prompted our old question, "Well, what's next?"

Papa handed me a small white envelope with a royal crest. I held it up, "What's this?"

He shrugged, his fingers urging me to open it. It held a small crisp white card embossed with a gold crown and a legend: His Royal Highness Leopold II, Kingdom de Belgique. *The King of Belgium?* Holy cow!

On the back was handwritten, "You are invited to Private Room 717 this evening."

Very well, I may be curious, but not foolhardy. I showed the card to Gerard and asked him to accompany me to Room 717. I slipped on my cape and hat as we walked around to the front of the house. Here I found the VIP Entrance and knocked at Private Room 717. A courtly manservant opened the door, and apparently expecting me, escorted us to what resembled a royal suite.

In a tall gold-sculptured chair sat a bearded old duffer in a distinguished civilian suit with two bearded aides at each side.

I bowed, "Your Majesty," and he arose to shake my hand, "*Bonsoir,* Monsieur Gassoon. Have a seat. Please. No need for royal formality; we are but strangers in a music hall. Care for some brandy?"

He signaled his manservant to pour drinks, and then presented his two companions: his nephew Archduke Frederick, and his aide de camp, Surgeon General Wilhelm Von Schweinhunt. In turn, I introduced the noted music critic, Gerard Deladier. Bows and handshakes were exchanged, and the King raised his glass.

"A toast, gentlemen. To the bravest and most humorous man in the city of Paris, to his honor, Gassoon the Great!" I thanked him as we sipped our brandy. I noticed that Gerard casually demurred, preferring to sniff his drink. Conversation turned to a series of compliments and questions.

"How do you do it? What is your secret, Monsieur Gassoon?" asked the King.

"Oh, but that would be telling a trade secret."

"A trade?" asked the King. "There are more such as you?"

"There are . . . many amateurs."

"Of course," said the General. "But you, you are one of a kind."

"Indeed," smiled his aide. "You are one fart—

"One smart feller!" snapped the king.

"I wonder," ventured the Archduke. "Might we see the rectal pore?"

A prickly feeling ran down my spine. Suddenly this was personal.

"Ta-ta, not possible. It is past closing hours."

"A mere peek at the stoma, just for his highness?"

It was highly personal. I was about to take my leave when I felt weak-kneed.

"I'm feeling ill. Perhaps another time. Gerard, lend a hand."

In a rush four pairs of hands were supporting me, lifting me onto a gurney table. "What the hell!?" All I could hear was Gerard's strong command—"Stand back! Let go, you bloody thieves! You'll get none of Gassoon's body parts tonight! Back, back!"

Above the hubbub rode the "King's" imperious voice, "How dare you! How dare you call us bloody thieves!?"

Gerard countered, "Your photos in tonight's newspapers say you are Nederland, Entwhistle, and Glomerulke, the Donor Organ Gang! Thieves of body parts.

You steal and sell body parts!"

Their servant made a move to lock the door. But Gerard rolled the gurney into his path—and then wheeled it at all three flesh peddlers. They were bowled over and Gerard was out the door carrying me on his back.

Later that night, about midnight, I roused myself from the drugged brandy and sat up in my dressing room. I felt somewhat torn between a hang-over and a Cat's Paw, a tool used to rip limbs from a body.

Immediately I called a meeting. In minutes I explained the situation to my staff. If they wished to quit, they would receive full separation pay. If they stayed on, we faced some dangers. "The Body Parts Gang will most likely pursue me, and I will have to find refuge for awhile, until they're caught."

"But where? Where's it safe?" asked Lee.

"I'll have to think. I know of no such place now."

"In Paris? I'd rather doubt it," said Papa.

"Then we'll have to search elsewhere. But quickly, I suspect they may have hidden a spy in our ranks."

"Yes, Jean! I'll take care of your funding," Oller agreed.

"Good, then let's get about it tonight. Papa and I will go scouting tomorrow morning. You, Monsieur Oller, will open a bank account, and secure our travel credentials.

Lee, you could gather up my supplies. But remember, friends, our deadline is here, tomorrow afternoon.

And that leaves a little time for us, Gerard."

When they had left, Gerard and I shared some private time

"Last night," I asked, "How did you know they were crooks?"

"I saw their photos in the Gazette. I assumed they were after your intestines and butt, Maybe more, your kidneys."

"Poor devils," I said, "Now they'll have to shop elsewhere, perhaps at Rodin's. I certainly thank you!"

"You're welcome, sir. But look—we both know they are persistent devils. And you can bet they'll be back, now or within days."

"Ah! This is exactly when your gendarmes must nab them. You can pave the way by being ready to arrest them. Where will I be? Maybe Corsica, Capri, Sicily? Perhaps at sea—who knows? Only you. We will have to be in touch with local gendarmes. Vive la France! Your contacts here will be Lee and my father. Any questions? Let's see how much we can get done by tomorrow afternoon."

Vive La Seine

Early Sunday morning Papa and I took the Metro to the Bastille stop. From there we walked to the Porte d'Arsenal. We knew a small boatyard near the river, and we started our search. They had all makes. A ketch, sloop, a trim skiff. But one boat caught my eye, a fairly good-sized dinghy, perhaps twelve or so feet. I looked it over and asked, "What condition is it in? Is it seaworthy?"

"Oh it could use a good cleaning, some paint. But the hull and motor and controls are in good order. Shipshape, as they say."

"I'm interested in about a month's rental. What would that run?"

"Oh, many francs. One month would run half a million francs just for the dinghy. Plus insurance. That would be another 500,000/six mo."

Fortunately, we brought cash, and said, "Yes, we could handle that. Probably here, today." A handshake and the deal was done.

Within an hour. I was chugging up the Seine, riding with the rushing Seine. While I was at the tiller, Papa was painting a sign, "Hey Jean! What name do you want?"

"None, no name." I answered.

And so we were on our way, off to a new adventure and hideout.

That afternoon we had finished our shake-down and were moored back at the Porte de l'Arsenal, quietly conferring with our inner circle.

"A good idea," judged Gerard, "Nobody'll think of you at sea."

He and Lee were pleased with the plan. "Whee! Next week we'll go on an excursion!" Without further ado, we shoved off on our river cruise.

The Seine's rushing waters helped us conserve petrol, and in a short while we were churning northwest toward Normandy, heading past Giverny and passing Evreux up toward Rouen. No question, the Seine runs a snaky course. But to us it became graceful, curving up through the villages of Les Andelys, and Lyons-la-Foret. Approaching Rouen it fanned out into a more gentle arc.

But no sooner did we enter the wider stream than we noticed the approach of a distant cigarette-type speedboat. At the helm we could discern three familiar bearded gents—the Belgian Body Parts Gang.

So this was it. We were to be overtaken by these bloodsuckers, body parts thieves out for human plunder. They'd laid back for some time, waiting for this clearing. Now it was up to us to make them regret every foot of water. Without a radio, gendarmes, signals or big burly sailors, we were kind of stuck. Our only ally would be our own wits. As the trio drew up to our port side, they hooked our dinghy with a grappling line and drew us close enough for two of them to leap aboard.

Timed with their leap, Papa jumped aboard their boat! With his machete, he swiped their line in two and turned to take on the pilot, the gent they called the King. One wave of Pop's machete was all it took. In terror the King bailed out into the Seine.

Nobody saw him surface so we assumed he swam like a lead weight. I yelled to Pop to take command of the speedboat and meet me in Paris, and I turned to deal with the two aides. What they hadn't realized was that the dinghy didn't smell from fresh paint. It had been soaked with petrol.

I smiled to the men. "So you'd like my body parts? My ass and intestines, eh? Well, how would you like them, grilled or sautéed?" With that I lit a matchbook and tossed it on deck.

The whole dinghy went up in a blaze, exploding the two crooks into space while I slipped into the Seine. A few yards of submerged swimming and I looked back at the wreckage of the doomed Donor Parts Gang. A wonderfully glowing sight.

That left only one last chore, getting back to Paris. Off came my breeches and drawers, and I pointed downstream. A gentle grunt started up fart propulsion. It would be a long hoe to row, but at last I was on my way, back to Paris, and a comedic career.

It must have been quite a sight for Rouen fishermen. First these boats collide, and a dignified old duffer dives into the Seine. Then the massive explosion of a dinghy followed by several flying sailors. A speedboat races away. And, now this! A naked butt bubbling this fellow downstream, put-put-put south toward Paris.

Truly, *le Fin de Siecle* is not over.

THE END

www.ingramcontent.com/pod-product-compliance
Lightning Source LLC
Chambersburg PA
CBHW021911040426
42447CB00007B/800